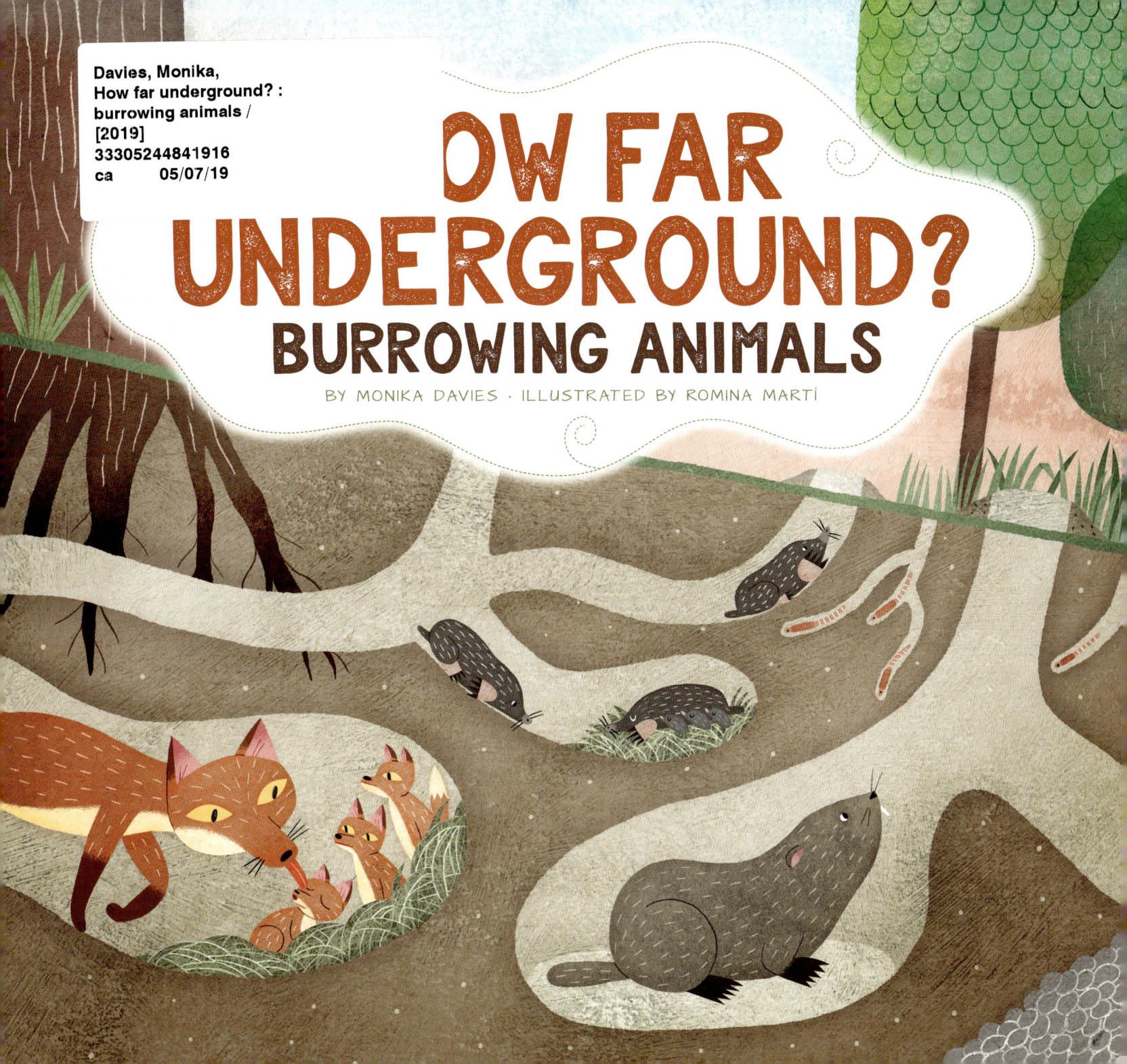

Amicus Illustrated
is published by Amicus and Amicus Ink.
P.O. Box 1329
Mankato, MN 56002
www.amicuspublishing.us

Copyright © 2019 Amicus. International copyright reserved in all countries. No part of this book may be reproduced in any form without written permission from the publisher.

Library of Congress Cataloging-in-Publication Data
Names: Davies, Monika, author. | Marti, Romina, illustrator.
Title: How far underground? : burrowing animals / by Monika Davies ; illustrated by Romina Marti.
Other titles: Burrowing animals
Description: Mankato, MN : Amicus Illustrated, [2019] | Series: Animals measure up | Audience: K to grade 3. | Includes bibliographical references.
Identifiers: LCCN 2017057757 (print) | LCCN 2017060821 (ebook) | ISBN 9781681514680 (pdf) | ISBN 9781681513867 (library binding) | ISBN 9781681523064 (pbk.)
Subjects: LCSH: Burrowing animals—Juvenile literature. | Animals—Habitations—Juvenile literature. | Animal behavior—Juvenile literature.
Classification: LCC QL756.15 (ebook) | LCC QL756.15 .D38 2019 (print) | DDC 591.56/48—dc23
LC record available at https://lccn.loc.gov/2017057757

Editor: Rebecca Glaser
Designer: Kathleen Petelinsek

Printed in the United States of America

HC 10 9 8 7 6 5 4 3 2 1
PB 10 9 8 7 6 5 4 3 2 1

About the Author

When she was young, Monika Davies wanted to live underground in a maze of tunnels—just like a red fox! Now, she likes to stay above ground where it is drier. Monika graduated from the University of British Columbia with a bachelor of fine arts in creative writing. She has written over eighteen books for young readers.

About the Illustrator

Romina Martí is an illustrator who lives and works in Barcelona, Spain, where her ideas come to life for all audiences. She loves to discover and draw all kinds of creatures from around the planet, who then become the main characters for the majority of her work. To learn more, go to: rominamarti.com

Not all creatures stay out in the sun. Some build their homes in the soil! These underground homes all look different. They are called burrows, and they give animals a place to hide. Down below, the animals lead secret lives.

The grasslands stretch far and wide. Here, the soil hides many animals. Moles are master diggers. They spend their lives in the soil.

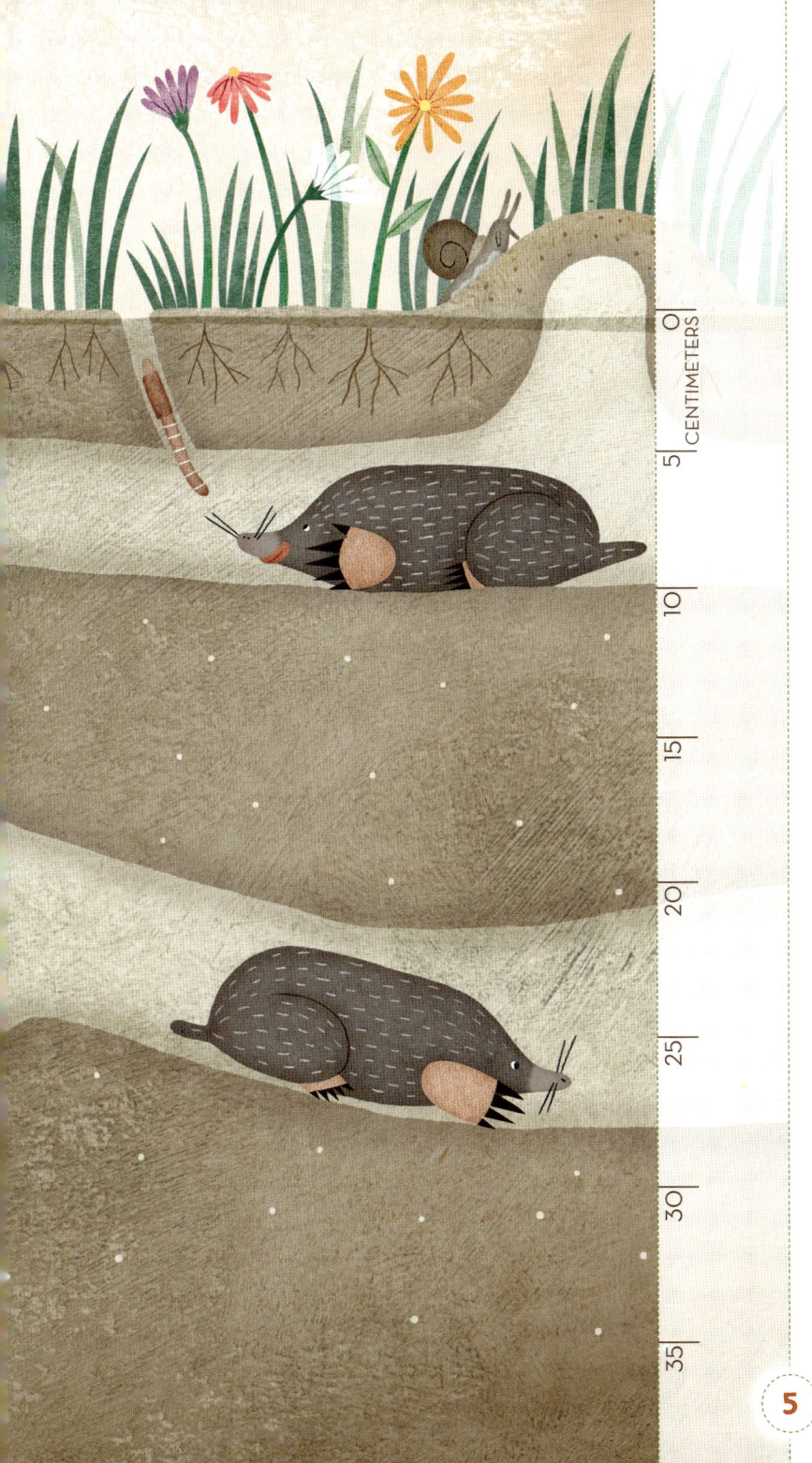

To move around, they dig tunnels. This maze of tunnels is their home. Their homes lie 12 inches (30.5 cm) below ground.

A mole's diet includes earthworms, which also tunnel through soil. Earthworms eat decaying plants and other things in the soil. If it is very dry, they can dig about 6.5 feet (2 m) down to find water.

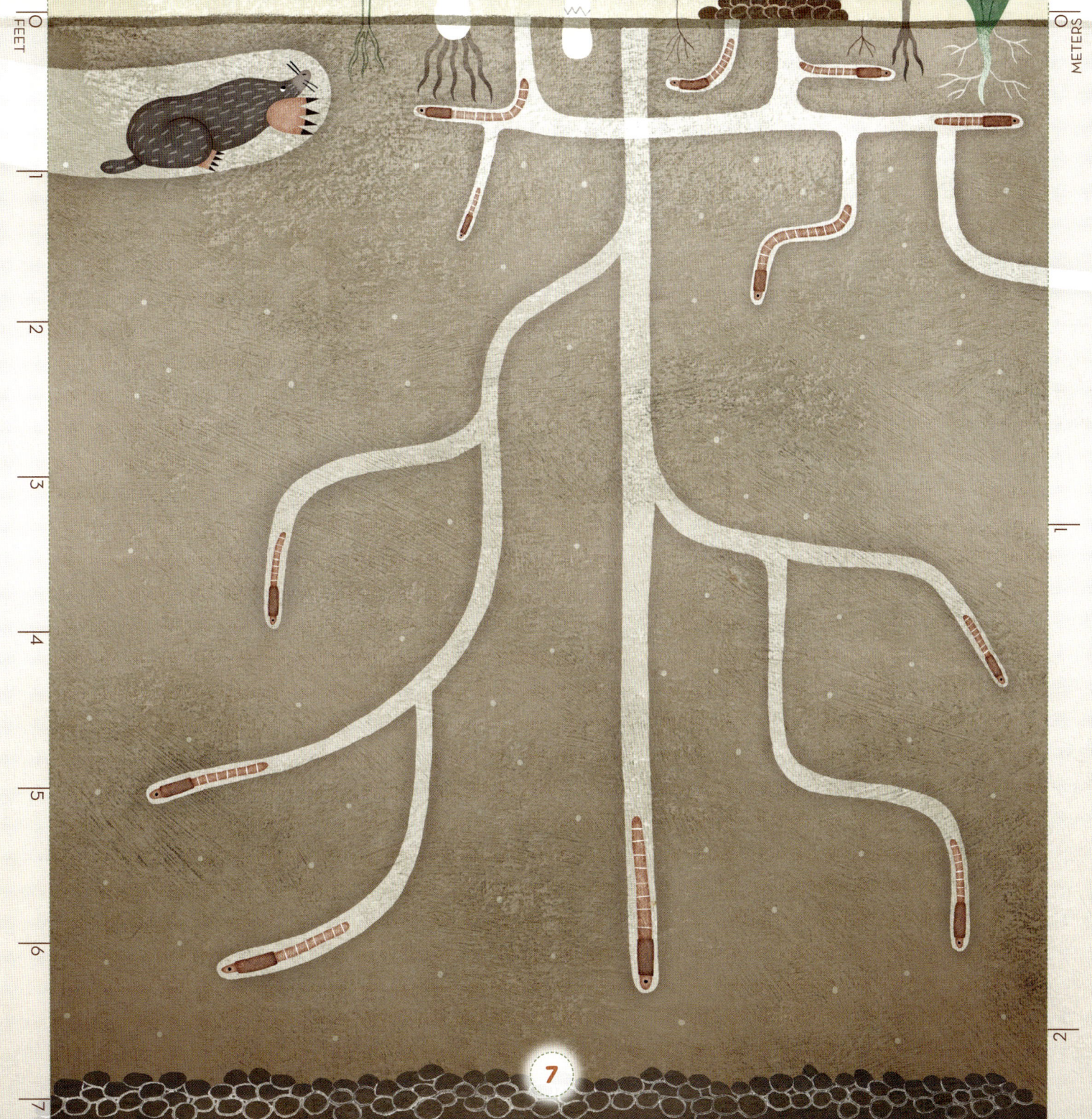

Groundhogs are slow runners. To stay safe, they must hide from enemies. Their burrows keep them unseen.

A groundhog's home goes deep into the soil. Their burrows have two or more entrances, so they have several escape routes.

If a groundhog moves out of its burrow, a red fox might move in! When it's time to have kits, the mother fox finds an old burrow that is already dug out.

Then, she makes it bigger. Some fox burrows can stretch to 75 feet (23 meters) long. That's longer than four minivans!

The dry, hot desert also hides burrows. Many animals need shelter from the harsh heat of the day. Desert tarantulas only come out at night. During the day, they tuck themselves into burrows just a few inches under the ground. They line their homes with silk. This keeps the burrow's walls from falling in.

Many frogs live in wet homes. But some frogs live in dry climates. In Australia, the Spencer's burrowing frog handles high heat by heading underground. Their burrows keep them shaded and cool. They stay there until it rains again.

South of the Sahara Desert, aardvarks live for the night. They are nocturnal animals. And they like to dig! Their strong arms and claws help them dig deep and find ants and termites to eat.

Meet the Jerboa mouse. It can leap away from predators! Sometimes, these mice dig a quick hole near the surface to hide. But their long-term homes go deep underground. These burrows are dug 8 feet (2.4 meters) below.

A burrow can also twist and twirl! The monitor lizard digs down in a spiral. At the bottom, the lizard lays its eggs. The burrow's shape confuses enemies. They can't find their way in! The eggs are safe.

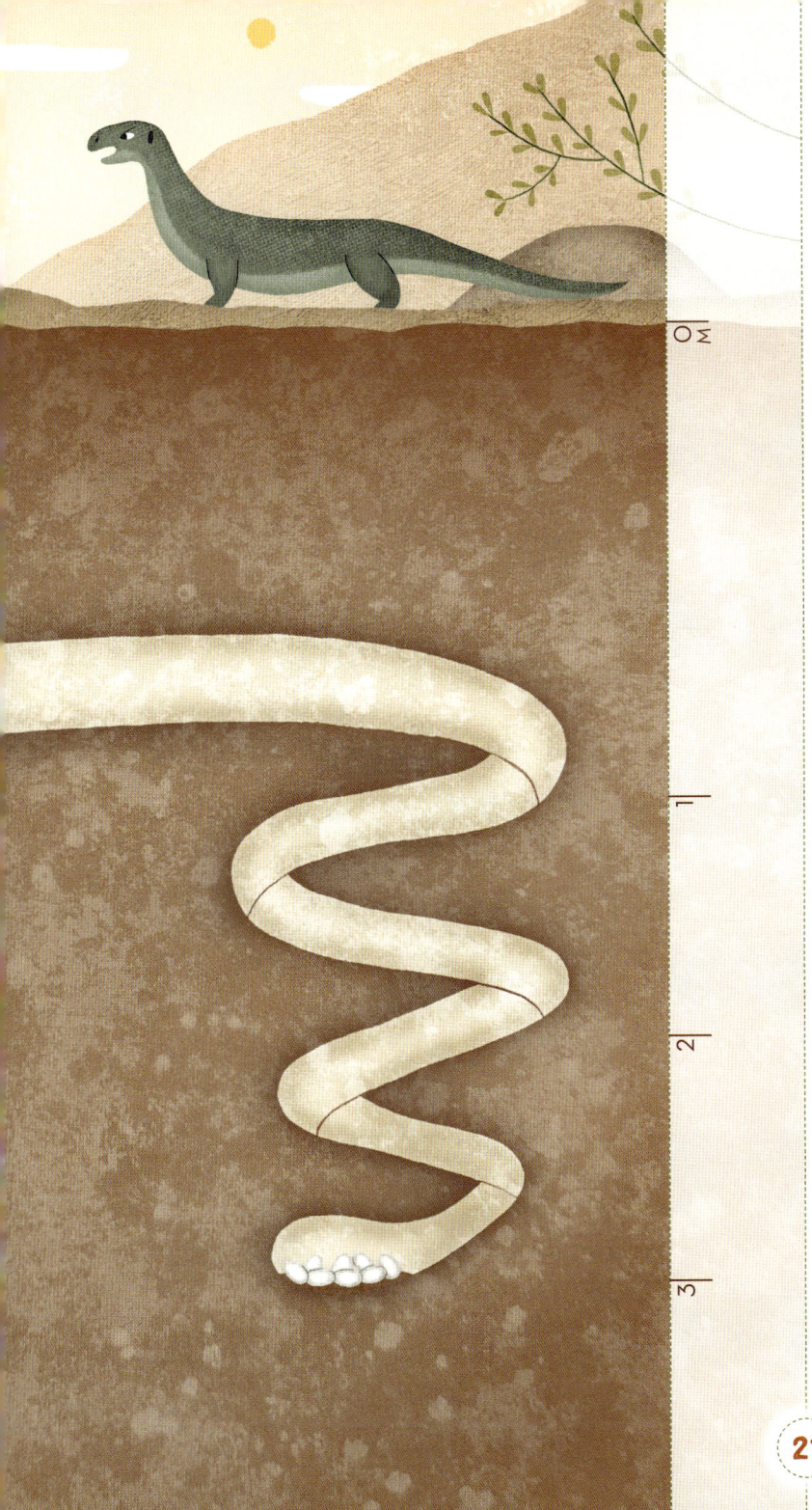

Burrowing animals build a life underground. There is another world under your feet!

GLOSSARY

burrow (noun) A hole or tunnel in the ground that an animal (such as a rabbit or fox) makes to live in or for safety.

burrow (verb) To make a hole or tunnel in the ground by digging.

climate The weather patterns and conditions of a region.

decay To rot or decompose.

nocturnal Active mainly at night.

READ MORE

Messner, Kate. **Up in the Garden and Down in the Dirt**. San Francisco: Chronicle Books, 2015.

Royston, Angela. **Animals that Dig**. Chicago: Capstone Raintree, 2014.

Schuetz, Kari. **Groundhogs**. Minneapolis: Bellwether Media, 2014.

WEBSITES

Beneath Your Feet – *Houghton Mifflin Science*

https://www.eduplace.com/kids/hmsc/k/b/cricket/ckt_kb.shtml

Explore the hidden world of animal homes "beneath your feet"!

BioKIDS: Kids' Inquiry of Diverse Species: Red Fox

http://www.biokids.umich.edu/critters/Vulpes_vulpes/

Read more about red fox behavior and why it makes burrows.

Groundhog: Burrow Mania!

https://kids.nationalgeographic.com/animals/groundhog/

Read about the groundhog's burrowing behaviors and look at photos of groundhogs.

Every effort has been made to ensure that these websites are appropriate for children. However, because of the nature of the Internet, it is impossible to guarantee that these sites will remain active indefinitely or that their contents will not be altered.